J R HARRIS

Use What You Don't Got to Get What You Want

Your Guide to Smart Land Flipping

Copyright © 2024 by J R Harris

All rights reserved. No part of this publication may be reproduced, stored or transmitted in any form or by any means, electronic, mechanical, photocopying, recording, scanning, or otherwise without written permission from the publisher. It is illegal to copy this book, post it to a website, or distribute it by any other means without permission.

J R Harris asserts the moral right to be identified as the author of this work.

J R Harris has no responsibility for the persistence or accuracy of URLs for external or third-party Internet Websites referred to in this publication and does not guarantee that any content on such Websites is, or will remain, accurate or appropriate.

Designations used by companies to distinguish their products are often claimed as trademarks. All brand names and product names used in this book and on its cover are trade names, service marks, trademarks and registered trademarks of their respective owners. The publishers and the book are not associated with any product or vendor mentioned in this book. None of the companies referenced within the book have endorsed the book.

First edition

This book was professionally typeset on Reedsy.
Find out more at reedsy.com

Contents

Use What You Don't Got to Get What You Want: Your Guide to...	1
Introduction	2
Chapter 1: Understanding Land Flipping	3
Chapter 2: Starting with Little Money	10
Chapter 3: Financing Strategies	18
Chapter 4: Flipping Land Without Owning It	28
Chapter 5: Flipping Land Through Tax Liens and Deeds	37
Chapter 6: Case Studies and Examples	47
Chapter 7: Common Pitfalls	55
Chapter 8: Legal Considerations	64
Chapter 9: Marketing Your Land	73
Conclusion	84
Helpful Websites	85

Use What You Don't Got to Get What You Want: Your Guide to Smart Land Flipping

Introduction

Welcome to "Use What You Don't Got to Get What You Want," your comprehensive guide to turning vacant plots into profit, even if you're starting with limited funds. Land flipping can be a lucrative venture, and this book will cover various strategies to help you enter the market, including innovative ways to flip land without actually owning it and leveraging tax liens and deeds to maximize your investment potential. You'll find practical advice, real-life examples, tips, and helpful resources throughout.

Chapter 1: Understanding Land Flipping

What is Land Flipping?

Land flipping is the process of purchasing land at a low price and selling it at a higher price to make a profit. Unlike house flipping, which involves renovating and reselling homes, land flipping typically does not require physical improvements to the property. This makes it an appealing option for investors who prefer a less hands-on approach.

Why Invest in Land?

Investing in land offers several advantages:

- **Lower Initial Costs:** Vacant land is generally less expensive than developed properties, making it accessible for investors with limited funds.
- **Less Competition:** The land market is often less competitive than the housing market, providing more opportunities for good deals.
- **Simplicity:** Land doesn't require maintenance, repairs, or dealing with tenants, reducing the complexities associated

with property management.
- **Appreciation Potential:** In growing areas, land can appreciate significantly over time, leading to substantial profits.

Types of Land for Flipping

Raw Land

- Undeveloped land with no structures or utilities.
- Often found in rural or undeveloped areas.
- Requires thorough research on zoning, land use, and future development plans.

Infill Lots

- Vacant lots located within developed urban or suburban areas.
- Typically easier to sell due to existing infrastructure and demand.
- Higher initial cost but quicker turnover potential.

Subdivision Lots

- Plots of land within a planned subdivision.
- May already have utilities and infrastructure in place.
- Attractive to developers and builders looking to construct new homes.

Factors Affecting Land Value

Understanding what influences land value is crucial for successful flipping. Here are key factors to consider:

Location

- Proximity to amenities, schools, and transportation.
- Future development plans for the area.
- Desirability of the neighborhood.

Zoning and Land Use

- Zoning regulations determine how land can be used (residential, commercial, agricultural, etc.).
- Verify zoning laws to ensure the intended use is permitted.
- Check for any planned changes in zoning that could affect the land's value.

Access and Utilities

- Availability of roads, water, electricity, and sewage systems.
- Easements or right-of-way issues that could impact access to the property.
- Costs associated with extending utilities to the property.

Topography and Soil Quality

- The land's physical characteristics, such as slope, drainage, and soil type.
- Suitability for construction or agriculture.

- Potential environmental issues like flood zones or contamination.

Market Demand

- Current demand for land in the area.
- Trends in real estate development and population growth.
- Economic conditions that could influence land prices.

Research and Due Diligence

Before purchasing land, thorough research and due diligence are essential to avoid costly mistakes. Here are steps to follow:

Property Research

- Obtain a title report to check for any liens, encumbrances, or legal issues.
- Verify the property boundaries through a survey.
- Investigate any environmental concerns, such as wetlands or contamination.

Market Analysis

- Analyze recent sales of comparable land in the area.
- Study the local real estate market trends and growth projections.
- Identify potential buyers and demand for the type of land you're considering.

Zoning and Permits

- Confirm the zoning classification and permissible uses of the land.
- Check for any required permits or approvals for your intended use.
- Understand any restrictions or covenants that may apply.

Access and Infrastructure

- Assess the accessibility of the land and availability of utilities.
- Calculate the costs of improving access or extending utilities if necessary.
- Identify any potential issues with easements or rights-of-way.

Building a Network

Successful land flipping often involves building a network of professionals who can provide valuable insights and assistance. Consider connecting with:

Real Estate Agents

- Agents specializing in land sales can help you find good deals and provide market insights.

Surveyors

- Professional surveyors can verify property boundaries and identify potential issues.

Attorneys

- Real estate attorneys can assist with legal matters, contracts, and due diligence.

Environmental Consultants

- Consultants can help assess any environmental risks or concerns.

Developers and Builders

- Networking with developers and builders can provide opportunities for partnerships or quick sales.

Case Study: Successful Land Flip

Scenario:

Emma, a new investor, purchased a 5-acre parcel of raw land in a rural area for $10,000. She researched the local zoning laws and discovered that the area was zoned for residential development. Emma learned of a planned highway extension nearby, which would significantly increase the land's value.

Steps Taken:

1. **Research:** Emma conducted thorough research on zoning,

future development plans, and market demand.
2. **Due Diligence:** She obtained a title report, verified property boundaries, and assessed access to utilities.
3. **Networking:** Emma connected with local real estate agents and developers to understand the market better.

Outcome:

Six months later, the highway extension was announced, and the land's value doubled. Emma sold the parcel for $25,000, making a $15,000 profit.

Tip:

Stay informed about local development plans and infrastructure projects that could impact land values.

Chapter 2: Starting with Little Money

Finding Affordable Land

Online Listings

- **Websites:** Explore websites like Zillow, LandWatch, and Craigslist to find affordable land listings. These platforms often have filters to help you find properties within your budget.
- **Tip:** Set up alerts for new listings that meet your criteria to stay ahead of the competition.

Auctions

- **Local Auctions:** Attend local property auctions, where you can often find land at lower prices. Check with your county or city for information on upcoming auctions.
- **Online Auctions:** Websites like Bid4Assets and Auction.com offer online land auctions, making it easier to find deals from the comfort of your home.

Networking

- **Real Estate Groups:** Join local real estate investment groups or online forums like BiggerPockets to connect with other investors. Networking can lead to finding off-market deals or partnerships.
- **Real Estate Agents:** Work with agents who specialize in land sales. They can provide insights into affordable properties and upcoming opportunities.

Direct Mail Campaigns

- **Targeting Owners:** Send direct mail letters to landowners in areas you're interested in. Some owners may be willing to sell their land at a discount, especially if they've been holding onto it without any plans for development.
- **Personalized Approach:** Customize your letters to address the owner's specific situation, and offer a quick and hassle-free sale process.

Example:

Tom found a seller willing to finance a piece of land with a $1,000 down payment and monthly payments.

Creative Financing Methods

Seller Financing

- **How It Works:** In seller financing, the seller acts as the lender, allowing the buyer to make payments over time instead of paying the full price upfront. This can be an

attractive option if you have trouble securing a traditional loan.
- **Benefits:** Easier qualification, flexible terms, and potentially lower interest rates.
- **Tip:** Negotiate favorable terms, such as a low down payment and an extended payment period.

Partnerships

- **Sharing Costs:** Partnering with other investors allows you to pool resources and share the costs of purchasing and holding land. This can be an effective way to start with limited funds.
- **Finding Partners:** Look for partners through real estate investment groups, online forums, or personal networks. Ensure that you clearly outline the terms of the partnership and each party's responsibilities.

Hard Money Loans

- **Short-Term Financing:** Hard money loans are short-term loans provided by private lenders. These loans are typically easier to obtain than traditional bank loans but come with higher interest rates.
- **Using Hard Money Loans:** Use hard money loans to finance the initial purchase of land, and then refinance or sell the property quickly to pay off the loan.

Lease Options

- **How It Works:** A lease option allows you to lease a piece of land with an option to purchase it later. This strategy enables you to control the property and potentially flip it for a profit without initially buying it outright.
- **Benefits:** Lower upfront costs and the ability to test the market before committing to a purchase.

Example:
Sarah leased a plot of land for $200/month with an option to buy. She found a buyer within six months and assigned the option for a $5,000 fee.

Negotiating Deals

Understanding Seller Motivation

- **Identify Motivations:** Understanding why a seller is looking to sell can help you negotiate better terms. Common motivations include financial distress, relocating, or simply wanting to offload unused land.
- **Tailored Offers:** Tailor your offers to address the seller's specific needs, such as offering a quick closing or flexible payment terms.

Making an Offer

- **Low Initial Offer:** Start with a low initial offer to leave room for negotiation. Be prepared to justify your offer with market data and comparable sales.

- **Highlight Benefits:** Emphasize the benefits of a quick and hassle-free sale, especially if you're working with motivated sellers.

Contingencies and Terms

- **Include Contingencies:** Include contingencies in your offer to protect yourself, such as a due diligence period or financing contingency.
- **Flexible Terms:** Be open to negotiating flexible terms, such as seller financing or extended closing periods.

Example:

Sarah leased a plot of land for $200/month with an option to buy. She found a buyer within six months and assigned the option for a $5,000 fee.

Managing Holding Costs

Understanding Holding Costs

- **Property Taxes:** Property taxes are a significant holding cost. Research the tax rates in the area before purchasing land and factor them into your budget.
- **Maintenance Costs:** While vacant land generally has lower maintenance costs than developed properties, there may still be expenses for clearing brush, maintaining access roads, or managing pests.
- **Utilities:** If utilities are available on the property, there may be minimal costs to keep them connected.

Minimizing Holding Costs

- **Buy and Flip Quickly:** The faster you can sell the property, the lower your holding costs will be. Focus on properties with high demand or in growing areas to ensure a quick sale.
- **Rent Out the Land:** Consider renting out the land for agricultural use, parking, or storage to generate income while you hold it.
- **Tax Strategies:** Explore tax strategies to minimize your property tax burden, such as applying for agricultural exemptions if applicable.

Building a Network

Real Estate Agents

- **Specialists in Land Sales:** Work with real estate agents who specialize in land sales. They can help you find affordable properties and provide valuable market insights.
- **Negotiating Deals:** Agents can assist with negotiating deals and handling paperwork, making the process smoother for beginners.

Surveyors

- **Verifying Property Boundaries:** Professional surveyors can verify property boundaries and identify any potential issues, such as encroachments or easements.
- **Conducting Surveys:** Conducting a survey before purchasing land can prevent legal disputes and ensure you're getting what you pay for.

Attorneys

- **Handling Legal Matters:** Real estate attorneys can assist with legal matters, such as reviewing contracts, conducting title searches, and ensuring compliance with zoning laws.
- **Protecting Your Interests:** Attorneys can help protect your interests and prevent costly legal issues down the road.

Environmental Consultants

- **Assessing Environmental Risks:** Environmental consultants can assess any environmental risks or concerns, such as soil contamination or proximity to wetlands.
- **Ensuring Compliance:** Consultants can ensure that your intended use of the land complies with environmental regulations.

Case Study: Starting Small and Scaling Up

Scenario:

Emily, a new investor, started with a small budget of $5,000. She joined a local real estate investment group and networked with experienced investors. Emily found a distressed property listed on Craigslist and negotiated a seller financing deal with a $1,000 down payment and monthly payments of $100.

Steps Taken:

1. **Research:** Emily conducted thorough research on the property and the local market.
2. **Negotiation:** She negotiated favorable terms with the seller, securing a low down payment and flexible payment

plan.
3. **Networking:** Emily leveraged her network to find potential buyers and marketed the property effectively.

Outcome:

Within six months, Emily sold the property for $10,000, making a $5,000 profit. She reinvested her profits into another property, gradually scaling up her investments.

Tip:

Start small and gradually scale up your investments as you gain experience and build your network.

Chapter 3: Financing Strategies

Understanding Financing Basics

Before diving into specific strategies, it's important to understand some basic principles of real estate financing:

Loan-to-Value (LTV) Ratio

- The LTV ratio is the ratio of the loan amount to the appraised value of the property. Lenders use this ratio to assess risk. Lower LTV ratios are generally considered less risky.
- **Example:** If you're buying land appraised at $100,000 and you need a $50,000 loan, the LTV ratio is 50%.

Interest Rates and Terms

- Interest rates are the cost of borrowing money, expressed as a percentage of the loan amount. Terms refer to the duration of the loan.
- Lower interest rates and longer terms can reduce monthly payments but may increase the total interest paid over the life of the loan.

Down Payments

- A down payment is an upfront payment made by the buyer. Higher down payments can lower the LTV ratio and may improve loan terms.
- **Example:** If you're purchasing land for $50,000 with a $10,000 down payment, you'll need to finance $40,000.

Seller Financing

What is Seller Financing?

- In seller financing, the seller acts as the lender, allowing the buyer to make payments over time instead of paying the full price upfront. This can be an attractive option if you have trouble securing a traditional loan.
- **Example:** You agree to purchase a $20,000 piece of land with a $2,000 down payment. The seller finances the remaining $18,000 at 5% interest over five years.

How to Find Seller-Financed Deals

- **Networking:** Talk to real estate agents, attend investment group meetings, and network with other investors to find sellers open to financing.
- **Direct Mail:** Send letters to landowners explaining your interest in buying and inquiring about seller financing options.
- **Online Listings:** Websites like Craigslist, LandWatch, and Zillow often list properties with seller financing options.

Negotiating Seller Financing

- **Interest Rates and Terms:** Negotiate a reasonable interest rate and loan term. Be prepared to offer a higher interest rate than traditional loans, as sellers are taking on more risk.
- **Down Payment:** Aim for a low down payment to conserve your cash. Explain how your plan to improve or flip the land will benefit both parties.
- **Payment Schedule:** Agree on a monthly payment schedule that fits your budget. Ensure the terms are clear in the contract.

Example:

Karen used a land contract to buy a piece of land, making monthly payments to the seller until the full amount was paid off.

Tip:

Negotiate favorable terms, such as low down payments and flexible payment schedules.

Crowdfunding

What is Crowdfunding?

- Crowdfunding involves raising small amounts of money from a large number of people, typically through online platforms. Real estate crowdfunding platforms allow investors to pool their money to finance property purchases.
- **Example:** You list your land flipping project on a crowdfunding site, and 100 people each invest $100, raising $10,000

for your purchase.

How to Use Crowdfunding for Land Flipping

- **Choosing a Platform:** Select a reputable crowdfunding platform like Fundrise, RealtyMogul, or Patch of Land. Each platform has different requirements and fees.
- **Creating a Pitch:** Develop a compelling pitch that outlines your project, including the location, potential returns, and your experience. Use high-quality images and detailed descriptions.
- **Setting Goals:** Determine your funding goal and how much equity you're willing to offer investors. Be clear about the timeline and expected returns.

Managing a Crowdfunded Project

- **Communication:** Maintain regular communication with your investors, providing updates on the project's progress and any changes to the timeline.
- **Financial Reporting:** Keep accurate financial records and provide periodic reports to investors. Transparency builds trust and encourages future investments.
- **Exit Strategy:** Clearly outline your exit strategy, whether it's selling the land, refinancing, or another approach. Ensure investors understand when and how they'll receive their returns.

Example:
Michael used a crowdfunding platform to raise $10,000 to buy and flip land, offering a percentage of the profits to investors.

Tip:
Create a compelling pitch and provide detailed information about the investment opportunity to attract backers.

Partnerships

Forming Partnerships

- Partnerships allow you to pool resources with other investors, sharing both the risks and rewards. This can be particularly useful if you lack the capital or experience to go it alone.
- **Example:** You and two other investors each contribute $5,000 to purchase a $15,000 plot of land. You share the profits equally after selling the land.

Finding Partners

- **Networking Events:** Attend real estate investment clubs, seminars, and local meetups to connect with potential partners.
- **Online Forums:** Participate in online real estate forums and social media groups to find like-minded investors.
- **Professional Contacts:** Leverage your existing professional network, including real estate agents, attorneys, and financial advisors, to find potential partners.

Structuring Partnerships

- **Roles and Responsibilities:** Clearly define each partner's role and responsibilities. For example, one partner might handle financing while another manages marketing.
- **Profit Sharing:** Agree on how profits will be distributed. This can be based on the amount of capital contributed or the value of each partner's efforts.
- **Legal Agreements:** Draft a partnership agreement outlining the terms of the partnership, including decision-making processes, dispute resolution, and exit strategies.

Example:
Lucy partnered with two other investors to purchase a larger plot of land than she could afford alone, splitting the profits after the sale.

Tip:
Clearly outline the terms of the partnership and responsibilities of each partner to avoid conflicts.

Private Money Lenders

What are Private Money Lenders?

- Private money lenders are individuals or companies that lend money based on the value of the property rather than the borrower's creditworthiness. These loans are often short-term and come with higher interest rates.
- **Example:** You secure a $50,000 loan from a private lender to purchase land, agreeing to repay the loan with interest within one year.

How to Find Private Money Lenders

- **Networking:** Connect with private lenders through real estate investment groups, online forums, and networking events.
- **Referrals:** Ask other investors for referrals to reliable private lenders they've worked with.
- **Online Platforms:** Use online platforms like LendingHome and Patch of Land to find private lenders.

Negotiating with Private Lenders

- **Interest Rates and Fees:** Expect higher interest rates than traditional loans, but negotiate to get the best terms possible. Be aware of any additional fees, such as origination fees or prepayment penalties.
- **Loan Terms:** Private loans are typically short-term, ranging from six months to a few years. Ensure the loan term aligns with your project timeline.
- **Repayment Plans:** Discuss repayment options, such as interest-only payments during the loan term with a balloon payment at the end.

Example:

Sam secured a loan from a private lender to buy a piece of land, offering a higher interest rate but more flexible repayment terms.

Tip:

Build relationships with private lenders and demonstrate your ability to successfully flip land to secure funding.

Using Home Equity

Home Equity Loans

- If you own a home with significant equity, you can use a home equity loan to finance your land purchase. A home equity loan allows you to borrow against the equity in your home, providing a lump sum to invest in land.
- **Example:** You have $100,000 in home equity and take out a $50,000 home equity loan to buy and develop land.

Home Equity Line of Credit (HELOC)

- A HELOC is a revolving line of credit secured by your home's equity. Unlike a home equity loan, a HELOC allows you to borrow only what you need, when you need it, up to a certain limit.
- **Example:** You have a $50,000 HELOC and use $20,000 to purchase land. You can borrow additional funds from the HELOC as needed.

Risks and Considerations

- **Risk to Your Home:** Using home equity for land investments puts your home at risk. If you can't repay the loan, you could lose your home.
- **Interest Rates:** Home equity loans and HELOCs often have lower interest rates than other types of financing, but rates can vary. Ensure you understand the terms before borrowing.
- **Loan Terms:** Understand the repayment terms and ensure

you can meet the payment schedule without compromising your financial stability.

Tip:

Carefully consider the risks before using home equity to finance land purchases. Ensure you have a solid plan for repayment and a clear strategy for your investment.

Government Programs

USDA Loans

- The U.S. Department of Agriculture (USDA) offers loans for purchasing rural land. These loans are designed to promote development in rural areas and often come with favorable terms.
- **Example:** You qualify for a USDA loan to purchase a rural plot of land, taking advantage of low interest rates and extended repayment terms.

SBA Loans

- The Small Business Administration (SBA) provides loans for land and real estate purchases if the land will be used for business purposes. SBA loans can be an excellent option for investors planning to develop commercial properties.
- **Example:** You obtain an SBA loan to purchase and develop a piece of land into a small business park.

Local Grants and Incentives

- Some local governments offer grants, tax incentives, or low-interest loans to encourage land development and investment in certain areas. Check with your local economic development office for available programs.
- **Example:** You receive a local grant to help cover the cost of infrastructure improvements on your land, reducing your overall investment cost.

Tip:

Research and take advantage of government programs and incentives that can reduce your financing costs and provide additional resources for your land investment projects.

Chapter 4: Flipping Land Without Owning It

Lease Options

What is a Lease Option?

- A lease option, also known as a rent-to-own agreement, involves leasing a piece of land with an option to purchase it later. This arrangement gives you control over the property and the right to buy it at a predetermined price within a specified period.
- **Example:** You lease a piece of land for $200 per month with the option to purchase it for $20,000 within two years.

Benefits of Lease Options

- **Low Initial Investment:** Lease options typically require a smaller initial investment compared to purchasing land outright.
- **Flexibility:** You can test the market and explore potential uses for the land without committing to a purchase.
- **Profit Potential:** If the land's value increases, you can

exercise your option to buy at the lower predetermined price and sell at a profit.

Steps to Implement a Lease Option

- **Identify Suitable Properties:** Look for properties where the owner may be open to a lease option arrangement. Motivated sellers, such as those facing financial difficulties or wanting to avoid foreclosure, are good candidates.
- **Negotiate Terms:** Discuss the lease terms, including monthly rent, option fee (a non-refundable fee for the right to purchase), purchase price, and option period. Ensure the terms are clearly outlined in a written agreement.
- **Market the Property:** While leasing the land, market it to potential buyers. Highlight the lease option terms and the benefits of buying the property at the predetermined price.
- **Exercise or Assign the Option:** If you find a buyer, you can either exercise the option to purchase the land and then sell it to the buyer, or assign the lease option contract to the buyer for a fee.

Example:
Sarah leased a plot of land for $200/month with an option to buy. She found a buyer within six months and assigned the option for a $5,000 fee.
Tip:
Negotiate lease terms that give you enough time to find a buyer.

Assignments

What is an Assignment?

- An assignment involves finding a good deal on a piece of land, getting the property under contract, and then assigning the contract to another buyer for a fee. This method allows you to profit from the deal without ever taking ownership of the land.
- **Example:** You find a piece of land under contract for $15,000 and assign the contract to another buyer for $20,000, making a $5,000 profit.

Benefits of Assignments

- **No Ownership Required:** You don't need to own the land, which eliminates the need for significant capital or financing.
- **Quick Profits:** Assignments can generate quick profits as the transaction is completed when you assign the contract.
- **Low Risk:** Since you don't own the land, your financial risk is minimized.

Steps to Implement an Assignment

- **Find a Good Deal:** Look for undervalued properties or motivated sellers willing to sell at a discount. Network with real estate agents, attend auctions, and search online listings.
- **Get the Property Under Contract:** Negotiate a purchase agreement with the seller. Ensure the contract includes

an assignment clause allowing you to assign the agreement to another buyer.
- **Market the Contract:** Find potential buyers interested in the property. Highlight the benefits and potential profits of purchasing the land at the agreed-upon price.
- **Assign the Contract:** Once you find a buyer, assign the purchase contract to them for a fee. Ensure the assignment agreement is clear and legally binding.

Example:
David found a land deal and assigned the contract to another investor for a $2,000 fee.
Tip:
Build a list of potential buyers to quickly assign contracts.

Wholesaling

What is Wholesaling?

- Wholesaling involves contracting a property at a lower price and selling the contract at a higher price. Similar to assignments, wholesaling allows you to profit from the deal without owning the land.
- **Example:** You contract a piece of land for $10,000 and sell the contract to a buyer for $15,000, making a $5,000 profit.

Benefits of Wholesaling

- **Minimal Investment:** Wholesaling requires minimal up-front capital since you don't need to purchase the land.
- **Fast Turnaround:** Wholesaling deals can be completed

quickly, often within days or weeks.
- **Scalability:** You can wholesale multiple properties simultaneously, increasing your profit potential.

Steps to Implement Wholesaling

- **Find Wholesale Deals:** Look for distressed properties, motivated sellers, or undervalued land. Use online listings, auctions, and direct mail campaigns to find deals.
- **Negotiate Purchase Agreements:** Negotiate a purchase agreement with the seller. Ensure the contract includes an assignment clause and a due diligence period.
- **Market the Property:** Market the property to potential buyers or investors. Highlight the property's value and potential profits.
- **Sell the Contract:** Assign the purchase contract to a buyer or use a double closing to complete the transaction. Ensure all legal and financial aspects are handled correctly.

Example:
Lisa wholesaled a plot of land, making a $3,000 profit without ever owning it.
Tip:
Focus on finding motivated sellers who need to sell quickly.

Bird-Dogging

What is Bird-Dogging?

- Bird-dogging involves finding potential real estate deals and referring them to other investors for a fee. As a bird dog, you act as a deal scout, identifying properties that fit specific criteria and passing the leads to investors.
- **Example:** You find a piece of land that meets an investor's criteria and refer it to them for a $1,000 referral fee.

Benefits of Bird-Dogging

- **No Capital Required:** Bird-dogging requires no capital investment as you don't need to purchase or contract the property.
- **Low Risk:** Since you don't own the land, your financial risk is minimal.
- **Networking Opportunities:** Bird-dogging helps you build relationships with investors and gain experience in the real estate market.

Steps to Implement Bird-Dogging

- **Understand Investor Criteria:** Connect with real estate investors and understand their criteria for potential deals, including location, price range, and property type.
- **Find Potential Deals:** Use online listings, auctions, and networking to find properties that meet the investors' criteria.
- **Verify Property Information:** Verify the property's details, including ownership, zoning, and market value. Ensure the information is accurate and reliable.

- **Refer the Deal:** Refer the property to the investor and provide all relevant information. Negotiate a referral fee and ensure the terms are clear.

Example:
John found a piece of land that matched an investor's criteria and referred it to them for a $500 fee.
Tip:
Build a network of reliable investors and understand their specific criteria to increase your chances of successful referrals.

Land Options

What is a Land Option?

- A land option gives you the right, but not the obligation, to purchase a piece of land at a predetermined price within a specified period. During the option period, you can market the property to potential buyers or investors.
- **Example:** You secure a land option for $1,000, giving you the right to buy the land for $50,000 within one year. If you find a buyer willing to pay $60,000, you can exercise the option and sell the land for a $10,000 profit.

Benefits of Land Options

- **Low Initial Cost:** Land options typically require a small option fee, minimizing your initial investment.
- **Flexibility:** You have the flexibility to exercise the option or let it expire, depending on market conditions and potential buyers.

- **Profit Potential:** If the land's value increases, you can profit by exercising the option and selling the land at a higher price.

Steps to Implement Land Options

- **Find Suitable Properties:** Look for properties where the owner is open to granting a land option. Motivated sellers and distressed properties are good candidates.
- **Negotiate Option Terms:** Negotiate the option fee, purchase price, and option period. Ensure the terms are clearly outlined in a written agreement.
- **Market the Property:** During the option period, market the property to potential buyers or investors. Highlight the benefits of buying the land at the predetermined price.
- **Exercise or Assign the Option:** If you find a buyer, you can either exercise the option to purchase the land and then sell it, or assign the land option contract to the buyer for a fee.

Example:

David secured a land option for $1,000, giving him the right to buy the land for $30,000 within six months. He found a buyer willing to pay $40,000 and exercised the option, making a $10,000 profit.

Tip:

Negotiate option terms that provide enough time to find a buyer and ensure the option fee is affordable.

Case Study: Successful Lease Option Flip

Scenario:

Emily, a new investor, wanted to start flipping land but didn't have enough capital to buy a property outright. She found a motivated seller who agreed to a lease option arrangement.

Steps Taken:

1. **Research:** Emily researched properties in her area and identified a piece of land with high potential for appreciation.
2. **Negotiation:** She negotiated a lease option agreement with the owner, securing a monthly lease of $200 and an option to buy the land for $20,000 within two years.
3. **Marketing:** Emily marketed the property to potential buyers, highlighting the lease option terms and the land's future development potential.
4. **Finding a Buyer:** Within six months, Emily found a buyer willing to pay $25,000 for the land. She assigned the lease option contract to the buyer for a $5,000 fee.

Outcome:

Emily successfully flipped the land without owning it, making a $5,000 profit with minimal upfront investment.

Tip:

Leverage lease options to control properties and profit from flipping land without significant capital investment.

Chapter 5: Flipping Land Through Tax Liens and Deeds

Understanding Tax Liens

What is a Tax Lien?

- A tax lien is a legal claim placed on a property by the government due to unpaid property taxes. When you purchase a tax lien, you pay the delinquent taxes on behalf of the property owner. In return, you receive interest on the amount paid, and if the owner fails to repay the taxes plus interest, you may be able to foreclose on the property.
- **Example:** John buys a tax lien certificate for $1,000, representing unpaid taxes on a piece of land. The owner must pay John $1,000 plus interest to clear the lien.

Benefits of Investing in Tax Liens

- **High Returns:** Tax liens often offer high-interest rates, providing a good return on investment if the owner redeems the property.
- **Low Cost of Entry:** You can purchase tax liens for relatively

low amounts, making it accessible for investors with limited funds.
- **Potential Ownership:** If the owner fails to redeem the lien, you may acquire the property at a significant discount.

Risks of Investing in Tax Liens

- **Property Condition:** The property may be in poor condition, requiring significant investment to make it marketable.
- **Redemption Period:** The redemption period, during which the owner can repay the taxes, can vary, leading to uncertainty about when you can foreclose.
- **Legal Complexities:** The foreclosure process can be legally complex and time-consuming.

How to Invest in Tax Liens

Research Local Laws and Procedures

- **Understand the Process:** Tax lien investing varies by state and county. Research local laws and procedures to understand how tax lien sales work in your area.
- **Redemption Period:** Determine the redemption period and the interest rates applicable to tax liens in your area.

Find Tax Lien Sales

- **County Tax Offices:** Check with your county tax office for information on upcoming tax lien sales. Many counties hold annual or semi-annual auctions.
- **Online Auctions:** Some counties offer online tax lien auc-

tions through platforms like Bid4Assets and RealAuction.

Evaluate Properties

- **Due Diligence:** Research the properties behind the tax liens. Verify property details, including location, condition, zoning, and market value.
- **Property Visit:** If possible, visit the properties to assess their condition and potential value.

Participate in Auctions

- **Register:** Register for the auction and understand the bidding process. Ensure you have the necessary funds available for bidding.
- **Bid Strategically:** Set a maximum bid based on your evaluation of the property's value and potential return on investment. Avoid overbidding, as it reduces your profit margin.

Managing Purchased Tax Liens

- **Monitor Redemptions:** Keep track of any redemptions and collect the principal plus interest if the owner repays the taxes.
- **Foreclosure:** If the owner fails to redeem the lien, initiate the foreclosure process to acquire the property. Consult with a real estate attorney to navigate the legal complexities.

Example:
Anna invested in a tax lien and made a 12% return when the

property owner paid off the taxes.
Tip:
Check local government websites for tax lien sale information.

Understanding Tax Deeds

What is a Tax Deed?

- A tax deed represents ownership of a property that has been sold by the government due to unpaid property taxes. When you purchase a tax deed, you buy the property outright, often at a fraction of its market value.
- **Example:** Mike bought a property at a tax deed auction for $2,000, gaining full ownership of the land.

Benefits of Investing in Tax Deeds

- **Immediate Ownership:** Unlike tax liens, tax deeds grant you immediate ownership of the property upon purchase.
- **Potential for High Profits:** You can acquire properties at significant discounts and sell them at market value for substantial profits.
- **Lower Competition:** There is often less competition at tax deed auctions compared to traditional real estate markets.

Risks of Investing in Tax Deeds

- **Property Condition:** The property may require significant repairs or improvements, which can be costly.
- **Title Issues:** There may be existing liens or encumbrances on the property that need to be resolved.

- **Marketability:** Some properties may be difficult to sell due to location or other factors.

How to Invest in Tax Deeds

Research Local Laws and Procedures

- **Understand the Process:** Tax deed sales procedures vary by state and county. Research local laws to understand how tax deed auctions work in your area.
- **Clear Title:** Ensure that the county provides a clear title upon purchase or understand the steps needed to clear any title issues.

Find Tax Deed Auctions

- **County Tax Offices:** Check with your county tax office for information on upcoming tax deed auctions. Many counties hold regular auctions.
- **Online Auctions:** Some counties offer online tax deed auctions through platforms like Auction.com and Bid4Assets.

Evaluate Properties

- **Due Diligence:** Research the properties available at the auction. Verify property details, including location, condition, zoning, and market value.
- **Property Visit:** If possible, visit the properties to assess their condition and potential value.

Participate in Auctions

- **Register:** Register for the auction and understand the bidding process. Ensure you have the necessary funds available for bidding.
- **Bid Strategically:** Set a maximum bid based on your evaluation of the property's value and potential return on investment. Avoid overbidding, as it reduces your profit margin.

Post-Purchase Steps

- **Clear Title:** Work with a title company or real estate attorney to clear any title issues and obtain a clear title for the property.
- **Property Improvement:** Assess the property's condition and make any necessary repairs or improvements to increase its market value.
- **Marketing and Sale:** Market the property to potential buyers through online listings, real estate agents, and local networks. Price the property competitively to ensure a quick sale.

Example:

Mike bought a property at a tax deed auction for $2,000 and sold it for $15,000.

Tip:

Attend local tax deed auctions to understand the process before bidding.

Hybrid Strategy: Combining Tax Liens and Tax Deeds

Diversify Investments

- Combine tax liens and tax deeds in your investment portfolio to diversify risk and increase profit potential. Tax liens offer high returns through interest, while tax deeds provide immediate ownership and potential for high profits.
- **Example:** Invest in a mix of tax liens for steady returns and tax deeds for potential windfall profits.

Leveraging Experience

- Use your experience with tax liens to identify high-potential properties for tax deed auctions. Conversely, leverage your knowledge of tax deed auctions to select tax liens on properties likely to go unredeemed.
- **Example:** John uses his success with tax liens to identify undervalued properties at tax deed auctions, maximizing his investment returns.

Case Study: Hybrid Strategy Success

Scenario:

Sarah, an experienced tax lien investor, decided to diversify her portfolio by participating in tax deed auctions. She researched properties with high potential and combined her knowledge of tax liens and tax deeds to make informed investment decisions.

Steps Taken:

1. Sarah invested in tax liens with high-interest rates and participated in tax deed auctions to acquire undervalued properties. She improved the properties and sold them for significant profits.
2. **Outcome:** Sarah achieved a balanced portfolio with steady returns from tax liens and high profits from tax deed sales, significantly increasing her overall investment returns.

Tip:

Diversify your investments by combining tax liens and tax deeds to balance risk and maximize profit potential.

Building a Network

Real Estate Agents

- **Specialists in Tax Sales:** Work with real estate agents who specialize in tax lien and tax deed sales. They can provide valuable insights and help you find profitable deals.
- **Negotiating Deals:** Agents can assist with negotiating deals and handling paperwork, making the process smoother for beginners.

Attorneys

- **Handling Legal Matters:** Real estate attorneys can assist with legal matters, such as reviewing contracts, conducting title searches, and ensuring compliance with local laws.
- **Protecting Your Interests:** Attorneys can help protect your interests and prevent costly legal issues during the foreclosure or title clearing process.

Title Companies

- **Clearing Titles:** Title companies can help clear any title issues and ensure you obtain a clear title upon purchasing a tax deed.
- **Title Insurance:** Consider purchasing title insurance to protect against future claims or title issues.

Contractors

- **Property Improvements:** Work with reliable contractors to assess and improve the condition of properties acquired through tax deeds, increasing their market value and appeal to buyers.
- **Cost Management:** Obtain multiple quotes and manage costs effectively to maximize your return on investment.

Case Study: Successful Tax Deed Flip

Scenario:

Emily, a new investor, wanted to start flipping land using tax deeds. She researched local tax deed auctions and identified a property with high potential.

Steps Taken:

1. **Research:** Emily researched properties available at the upcoming tax deed auction, focusing on undervalued land with high growth potential.
2. **Auction Participation:** She registered for the auction and set a maximum bid based on her evaluation of the property's value and potential return on investment.

3. **Winning the Bid:** Emily won the auction with a bid of $5,000, acquiring the property at a significant discount.
4. **Property Improvement:** She assessed the property's condition and made necessary improvements, including clearing brush and improving access roads.
5. **Marketing and Sale:** Emily marketed the property through online listings and local real estate agents, highlighting its potential for residential development.

Outcome:

Within six months, Emily sold the property for $20,000, making a $15,000 profit.

Tip:

Leverage local tax deed auctions to acquire undervalued properties and maximize your profit potential through strategic improvements and effective marketing.

Chapter 6: Case Studies and Examples

Case Study 1: Turning Raw Land into Profitable Lots

Scenario:

John, a novice investor, wanted to break into the land flipping market with a limited budget. He identified a large parcel of raw land in a growing suburban area.

Steps Taken:

1. **Research:** John spent several weeks researching local zoning laws, market trends, and future development plans. He discovered that the area was slated for residential expansion.
2. **Purchase:** He purchased a 10-acre plot for $30,000, using a combination of savings and a small personal loan.
3. **Subdivision:** John worked with a surveyor and local planning department to subdivide the 10-acre plot into smaller, more marketable residential lots.
4. **Infrastructure Improvements:** He invested in basic infrastructure improvements, such as access roads and utility hookups, to increase the lots' appeal to potential buyers.
5. **Marketing:** John listed the individual lots on multiple real

estate platforms and worked with a local real estate agent to attract buyers.

Challenges:

- **Regulatory Hurdles:** Navigating local zoning and planning regulations required time and effort.
- **Infrastructure Costs:** Funding the infrastructure improvements stretched John's budget, but he managed to secure a short-term loan to cover these expenses.

Outcome:

Within 18 months, John sold all the subdivided lots for a total of $75,000, making a net profit of $35,000 after all expenses. This successful flip gave him the capital and confidence to pursue more significant projects.

Tip:

Researching future development plans and working with local authorities can help you identify high-potential areas and navigate regulatory requirements effectively.

Case Study 2: Flipping Land through Tax Deed Auctions

Scenario:

Emily, an experienced real estate investor, decided to explore tax deed auctions as a new avenue for land flipping.

Steps Taken:

1. **Preparation:** Emily attended several tax deed auctions as an observer to understand the process. She also consulted with a real estate attorney to learn about legal considera-

tions.
2. **Identifying Properties:** She identified a list of properties with potential for significant appreciation. One particular property, a 2-acre lot in a rural area, caught her attention due to its low starting bid.
3. **Bidding:** At the auction, Emily successfully bid $5,000 for the property, which had an estimated market value of $25,000.
4. **Property Enhancement:** After acquiring the property, Emily hired a contractor to clear overgrown vegetation and improve access roads.
5. **Marketing:** She marketed the property through online platforms, emphasizing its potential for agricultural use or as a rural retreat.

Challenges:

- **Due Diligence:** Conducting thorough due diligence on the properties available at auction required significant effort.
- **Clearing Title:** Ensuring the title was clear of any encumbrances was a complex process that required professional assistance.

Outcome:

Emily sold the property within six months for $20,000, realizing a profit of $15,000. This experience motivated her to continue exploring tax deed auctions for future investments.

Tip:

Attending auctions as an observer and consulting with professionals can help you understand the process and mitigate risks associated with tax deed investments.

Case Study 3: Wholesaling Rural Land

Scenario:

David, a real estate agent, wanted to leverage his network and market knowledge to start wholesaling land.

Steps Taken:

1. **Building a Network:** David used his existing network of investors and buyers to gauge interest in rural land properties.
2. **Finding Deals:** He identified a 50-acre rural property listed at $100,000, significantly below market value due to the seller's financial distress.
3. **Contract Negotiation:** David negotiated a purchase agreement with the seller, securing the property for $90,000 with a 30-day closing period.
4. **Marketing the Contract:** He immediately marketed the contract to his network, offering it for $110,000. His marketing highlighted the property's potential for agricultural development and recreational use.
5. **Assigning the Contract:** Within two weeks, David found a buyer willing to purchase the contract for $110,000. He assigned the purchase agreement to the buyer, who completed the transaction.

Challenges:

- **Finding Buyers:** Finding the right buyer quickly was crucial to ensure the wholesaling deal closed within the contract period.
- **Contract Clarity:** Ensuring the purchase agreement and

assignment contract were legally sound required careful attention to detail.

Outcome:

David earned a $20,000 assignment fee, with minimal upfront investment. This successful wholesale deal encouraged him to pursue more opportunities and expand his wholesaling business.

Tip:

Leveraging your existing network and ensuring clear, legally sound contracts can help you successfully wholesale land with minimal risk and investment.

Case Study 4: Lease Option for Urban Infill Lots

Scenario:

Sarah, a young investor, wanted to enter the land market in urban areas but lacked the capital to purchase outright.

Steps Taken:

1. **Identifying Opportunities:** Sarah targeted urban infill lots, which are vacant parcels in already developed areas. She found a lot in a desirable neighborhood with potential for residential development.
2. **Negotiating Lease Option:** She negotiated a lease option with the property owner, agreeing to lease the lot for $300 per month with the option to buy it for $50,000 within two years.
3. **Securing a Buyer:** Sarah marketed the lot to local developers and investors, highlighting its prime location and development potential.

4. **Assigning the Option:** Within a year, she found a developer interested in the lot. Sarah assigned her lease option to the developer for a $10,000 fee.

Challenges:

- **Finding the Right Property:** Identifying desirable urban infill lots required extensive research and networking.
- **Marketing the Lease Option:** Effectively marketing the lease option to potential buyers took time and effort.

Outcome:

Sarah made a $10,000 profit through the lease option assignment, allowing her to reinvest in more lease options and gradually build her capital.

Tip:

Urban infill lots can offer high potential for lease options. Focus on desirable locations and effectively market the opportunity to developers and investors.

Case Study 5: Bird-Dogging for Experienced Investors

Scenario:

Tom, a beginner with no capital, wanted to break into real estate investing by bird-dogging for experienced investors.

Steps Taken:

1. **Building a Network:** Tom attended local real estate meetups and joined online forums to connect with experienced investors looking for property leads.
2. **Finding Deals:** He spent time researching online listings,

attending auctions, and driving through neighborhoods to identify potential investment properties.
3. **Verifying Information:** Tom verified property details, including ownership, zoning, and market value, to ensure the leads were reliable.
4. **Referring Leads:** He referred high-potential properties to investors in his network, negotiating a referral fee for each successful deal.

Challenges:

- **Establishing Trust:** Building trust with experienced investors took time and required proving the quality of his leads.
- **Research Effort:** Conducting thorough research to verify property details was time-consuming but essential for success.

Outcome:
Tom earned referral fees ranging from $500 to $1,500 per lead, generating a steady income while learning about real estate investing. This experience gave him the confidence and knowledge to eventually start his own investments.

Tip:
Focus on building trust and providing high-quality, verified leads to establish yourself as a reliable bird dog and generate income without capital investment.

Learning from Failures

Importance of Due Diligence

- **Case Study:** Jane rushed into purchasing a tax lien without thorough research. The property was in a flood zone and had significant environmental issues, leading to unexpected expenses and a loss.
- **Lesson Learned:** Always conduct thorough due diligence to identify potential risks and avoid costly mistakes.

Understanding Market Trends

- **Case Study:** Mike invested in rural land without understanding the local market. The area had declining property values, making it difficult to sell the land at a profit.
- **Lesson Learned:** Research local market trends and future development plans to ensure your investment has potential for appreciation.

Clear Contracts

- **Case Study:** Sarah entered into a lease option agreement with unclear terms, leading to a legal dispute with the property owner. The dispute delayed the sale and reduced her profit.
- **Lesson Learned:** Ensure all contracts are clear, legally sound, and reviewed by a real estate attorney to prevent misunderstandings and legal issues.

Chapter 7: Common Pitfalls

Overpaying for Land

Lack of Market Research

- **Problem:** Without thorough market research, you risk overpaying for land. Overpaying reduces your profit margin and can lead to financial losses.
- **Solution:** Always conduct detailed market research. Analyze recent sales data, compare prices of similar properties, and understand the local market trends.

Emotional Decisions

- **Problem:** Emotional decisions can lead to overpaying. Falling in love with a property or feeling pressured to close a deal quickly can cloud your judgment.
- **Solution:** Stay objective. Base your decisions on data and analysis rather than emotions. Set a maximum bid or purchase price and stick to it.

Inaccurate Valuations

- **Problem:** Relying on inaccurate or outdated valuations can lead to overpaying. Property values can fluctuate, and an inaccurate assessment can mislead you.
- **Solution:** Use multiple sources to determine property values, including professional appraisals, online valuation tools, and local real estate agents. Regularly update your valuations to reflect current market conditions.

Ignoring Zoning Laws and Restrictions

Zoning Regulations

- **Problem:** Ignoring zoning regulations can result in purchasing land that cannot be used for your intended purpose. This can lead to legal issues and financial losses.
- **Solution:** Research local zoning laws before purchasing. Ensure that the land is zoned for your intended use and understand any restrictions or requirements.

Land Use Restrictions

- **Problem:** Land use restrictions, such as environmental regulations or easements, can limit how you can use or develop the property.
- **Solution:** Check for any land use restrictions by consulting local planning departments, reviewing title reports, and conducting thorough due diligence.

Future Zoning Changes

- **Problem:** Future zoning changes can impact your investment. Land that is currently zoned favorably may be rezoned, affecting its value and usability.
- **Solution:** Stay informed about local planning and development initiatives. Engage with local planning departments and attend public meetings to understand potential future changes.

Underestimating Holding Costs

Property Taxes

- **Problem:** Underestimating property taxes can lead to unexpected expenses. High property taxes can significantly impact your holding costs and overall profitability.
- **Solution:** Research property tax rates in the area before purchasing. Factor these costs into your budget and investment calculations.

Maintenance and Upkeep

- **Problem:** Vacant land may still require maintenance, such as clearing brush, maintaining access roads, or managing pests. Failing to account for these costs can reduce your profit margins.
- **Solution:** Budget for ongoing maintenance costs. Consider hiring a property management company or contractors to handle maintenance tasks.

Utilities and Infrastructure

- **Problem:** Extending utilities and improving infrastructure can be costly. Failing to account for these expenses can lead to financial strain.
- **Solution:** Assess the availability and condition of utilities and infrastructure before purchasing. Budget for any necessary improvements and factor these costs into your investment analysis.

Failing to Conduct Proper Due Diligence

Title Issues

- **Problem:** Title issues, such as unresolved liens or encumbrances, can complicate your ownership and ability to sell the property.
- **Solution:** Conduct a thorough title search before purchasing. Consider purchasing title insurance to protect against future claims.

Environmental Concerns

- **Problem:** Environmental issues, such as contamination or proximity to hazardous sites, can impact the usability and value of the land.
- **Solution:** Perform an environmental assessment to identify any potential concerns. Consult with environmental professionals if necessary.

Legal and Regulatory Compliance

- **Problem:** Failing to comply with legal and regulatory requirements can lead to fines, legal disputes, and delays.
- **Solution:** Consult with a real estate attorney to ensure compliance with all applicable laws and regulations. Review contracts, permits, and other legal documents thoroughly.

Lack of Exit Strategy

Undefined Goals

- **Problem:** Without clear goals, you may struggle to determine when and how to sell the property. This can lead to missed opportunities and reduced profitability.
- **Solution:** Define your investment goals from the outset. Determine your target profit margin, holding period, and preferred exit strategy.

Market Timing

- **Problem:** Selling at the wrong time can impact your returns. Market conditions can fluctuate, affecting property values and buyer demand.
- **Solution:** Monitor market trends and adjust your exit strategy accordingly. Be prepared to hold the property longer if market conditions are unfavorable.

Inadequate Marketing

- **Problem:** Poor marketing efforts can result in a prolonged sales process and lower sale prices.
- **Solution:** Develop a comprehensive marketing plan. Utilize online platforms, real estate agents, and local networks to reach potential buyers.

Inadequate Financing Planning

Insufficient Capital

- **Problem:** Running out of capital can halt your investment plans and lead to financial strain.
- **Solution:** Ensure you have sufficient capital to cover the purchase, holding costs, and any necessary improvements. Consider multiple financing options and secure backup funding sources.

High-Interest Loans

- **Problem:** High-interest loans can eat into your profits, making the investment less viable.
- **Solution:** Shop around for the best loan terms. Consider alternative financing options such as seller financing, partnerships, or crowdfunding.

Cash Flow Management

- **Problem:** Poor cash flow management can lead to difficulties in covering expenses and servicing debt.
- **Solution:** Create a detailed cash flow plan. Monitor your income and expenses regularly and adjust your budget as needed.

Lack of Experience and Knowledge

Inadequate Training

- **Problem:** Lack of experience and knowledge can lead to poor decision-making and increased risk.
- **Solution:** Invest in education and training. Attend real estate courses, workshops, and seminars. Join real estate investment groups and seek mentorship from experienced investors.

Overreliance on Others

- **Problem:** Relying too heavily on others, such as real estate agents or contractors, without understanding the basics can lead to mistakes and mismanagement.
- **Solution:** Take the time to learn the fundamentals of land flipping. Stay involved in all aspects of your investment and make informed decisions.

Avoiding Risk Management

- **Problem:** Ignoring risk management can result in significant losses and setbacks.
- **Solution:** Identify potential risks and develop strategies to mitigate them. Diversify your investments, conduct thorough due diligence, and maintain a contingency fund.

Case Study: Avoiding Common Pitfalls

Scenario:

Mike, a new investor, wanted to flip land but lacked experience. He purchased a property without conducting thorough due diligence and encountered several issues.

Steps Taken:

1. **Research and Due Diligence:** Mike neglected to conduct a thorough title search and environmental assessment. After purchasing the property, he discovered unresolved liens and contamination issues.
2. **Financing Challenges:** He underestimated the holding costs and ran out of capital, forcing him to take out high-interest loans.
3. **Market Understanding:** Mike purchased the property without understanding the local market trends, leading to difficulty in selling the land at a profit.

Outcome:

Mike faced significant financial losses and legal challenges. He decided to educate himself on land flipping, attended real estate courses, and sought mentorship from experienced investors. With improved knowledge and strategies, Mike successfully flipped his next property.

Lesson Learned:

Conduct thorough research and due diligence, secure adequate financing, and continuously educate yourself to avoid common pitfalls in land flipping.

Chapter 8: Legal Considerations

Understanding Contracts

Purchase Agreements

- **Key Elements:** A purchase agreement is a legal document outlining the terms and conditions of the sale. It should include the purchase price, property description, contingencies, and closing date.
- **Contingencies:** Include contingencies that allow you to back out of the deal if certain conditions aren't met, such as obtaining financing, satisfactory inspection results, or clear title.
- **Review:** Always review the purchase agreement thoroughly. Consider having a real estate attorney review the document to ensure your interests are protected.

Assignment Contracts

- **Purpose:** Assignment contracts allow you to transfer your interest in a purchase agreement to another buyer. This is common in wholesaling.

- **Key Elements:** The contract should specify the original purchase agreement terms, the assignment fee, and the responsibilities of each party.
- **Legal Considerations:** Ensure the original purchase agreement permits assignment. Include a clause that absolves you of liability after the assignment is completed.

Lease Options

- **Structure:** A lease option agreement combines a lease contract with an option to purchase the property at a later date.
- **Key Elements:** Include the lease terms, option fee, purchase price, and the option period.
- **Protection:** Ensure the agreement specifies what happens if either party fails to meet their obligations. Clarify who is responsible for property maintenance during the lease period.

Example:

Sarah leased a plot of land for $200/month with an option to buy. She found a buyer within six months and assigned the option for a $5,000 fee.

Tip:

Negotiate lease terms that give you enough time to find a buyer.

Title Issues and Title Insurance

Conducting a Title Search

- **Purpose:** A title search investigates the history of the property's ownership to ensure there are no legal issues, such as liens or encumbrances, that could affect your ownership.
- **Process:** Hire a title company or real estate attorney to conduct the title search. They will review public records to confirm the seller's ownership and identify any claims against the property.
- **Common Issues:** Be aware of issues like unpaid property taxes, mortgages, easements, and judgments that can complicate ownership.

Title Insurance

- **Purpose:** Title insurance protects against financial loss from defects in the title that were not discovered during the title search.
- **Types of Coverage:** There are two main types of title insurance: lender's title insurance (protects the lender) and owner's title insurance (protects the buyer).
- **Benefits:** Title insurance covers legal fees and financial losses if a title defect is discovered after the purchase.

Example:
David purchased a property with a clouded title, meaning there were unresolved claims or liens against it, complicating his ability to sell the land.

Tip:
Perform a thorough title search and consider purchasing title insurance to protect against future claims.

CHAPTER 8: LEGAL CONSIDERATIONS

Zoning and Land Use Regulations

Understanding Zoning Laws

- **Purpose:** Zoning laws dictate how a piece of land can be used. Common zoning classifications include residential, commercial, industrial, and agricultural.
- **Research:** Check local zoning laws to ensure your intended use of the land is permitted. Contact the local planning or zoning department for information.
- **Zoning Changes:** Be aware of potential zoning changes that could impact your investment. Engage with local planning meetings and stay informed about development plans.

Land Use Permits

- **Purpose:** Depending on the intended use of the land, you may need to obtain various permits, such as building permits, environmental permits, or special use permits.
- **Process:** Submit permit applications to the relevant local authorities. Ensure all required documents and fees are included.
- **Compliance:** Follow all regulations and requirements associated with the permits to avoid legal issues and fines.

Example:
Robert failed to check zoning laws and bought land unsuitable for his plans, losing money.
Tip:
Consult with a real estate attorney to ensure compliance with all applicable zoning laws and land use regulations.

Environmental Regulations

Environmental Assessments

- **Purpose:** Environmental assessments evaluate the potential environmental risks associated with a property, such as contamination or proximity to hazardous sites.
- **Types:** Phase I Environmental Site Assessment (ESA) is a common initial assessment. If issues are found, a Phase II ESA may be required for further investigation.
- **Hiring Professionals:** Hire a qualified environmental consultant to conduct the assessment and provide a detailed report.

Environmental Regulations

- **Compliance:** Ensure your intended use of the land complies with federal, state, and local environmental regulations. Common regulations include the Clean Water Act, Clean Air Act, and Endangered Species Act.
- **Mitigation:** If environmental issues are found, you may need to develop a mitigation plan to address them. This could include cleanup efforts, habitat restoration, or other measures.

Example:
Sarah purchased land near a wetland area without realizing it was subject to strict environmental regulations, preventing her from developing the property as planned.

Tip:
Perform an environmental assessment to identify any poten-

tial concerns and ensure compliance with all regulations.

Legal Disputes and Resolution

Boundary Disputes

- **Common Issues:** Boundary disputes can arise when neighboring property owners disagree on the property lines. This can lead to legal conflicts and potential financial losses.
- **Resolution:** Conduct a professional survey to confirm property boundaries. If a dispute arises, attempt to resolve it amicably through negotiation or mediation. If necessary, seek legal assistance.

Contract Disputes

- **Common Issues:** Disputes can arise from misunderstandings or breaches of contract terms. This can delay transactions and lead to legal action.
- **Resolution:** Ensure all contracts are clear and comprehensive. If a dispute occurs, seek resolution through negotiation or mediation. Consult with a real estate attorney if the issue escalates.

Tenant Issues

- **Common Issues:** If you lease the land, disputes with tenants can arise over lease terms, property maintenance, or other issues.
- **Resolution:** Have a clear lease agreement outlining the responsibilities of both parties. Address any issues promptly

and professionally. Consider legal action if disputes cannot be resolved amicably.

Example:
Mike bought a piece of land only to find out later that there was a boundary dispute with a neighbor, leading to costly legal battles.
Tip:
Conduct a professional survey to confirm property boundaries before finalizing any purchase.

Managing Liability

Liability Insurance

- **Purpose:** Liability insurance protects you against claims resulting from injuries or damages that occur on your property.
- **Types:** General liability insurance covers a broad range of risks. Additional coverage, such as umbrella policies, can provide extra protection.
- **Choosing a Policy:** Work with an insurance agent to determine the appropriate coverage for your investment properties.

Creating Legal Entities

- **Purpose:** Forming a legal entity, such as a Limited Liability Company (LLC), can protect your personal assets from liability.
- **Benefits:** An LLC separates your personal and business

assets, limiting your personal liability in case of legal action.
- **Formation:** Consult with a legal professional to form an LLC and ensure compliance with all state and federal requirements.

Example:

Tom purchased a liability insurance policy and formed an LLC to protect his personal assets when investing in land.

Tip:

Consider liability insurance and forming a legal entity to protect your personal assets and manage liability risks.

Case Study: Navigating Legal Challenges

Scenario:

Jane, a new investor, faced multiple legal challenges when flipping land. She encountered zoning issues, a boundary dispute, and environmental concerns.

Steps Taken:

1. **Zoning Issues:** Jane purchased land without checking the zoning laws. She consulted with a real estate attorney to rezone the property for her intended use, but this delayed her project and increased costs.
2. **Boundary Dispute:** A neighbor claimed part of Jane's land as their own. Jane hired a surveyor to confirm the boundaries and resolved the dispute through mediation.
3. **Environmental Concerns:** An environmental assessment revealed contamination on the property. Jane developed a mitigation plan with the help of environmental consultants and obtained the necessary permits for cleanup.

Outcome:

Despite the challenges, Jane successfully navigated the legal issues and sold the property for a profit. The experience taught her the importance of thorough due diligence and legal compliance.

Lesson Learned:

Conduct thorough research, seek professional advice, and ensure compliance with all legal requirements to avoid costly legal challenges in land flipping.

Chapter 9: Marketing Your Land

Creating a Marketing Plan

Define Your Target Market

- **Identify Potential Buyers:** Determine who your potential buyers are. This could include developers, investors, farmers, or individuals looking to build their own homes.
- **Buyer Profiles:** Create profiles of your target buyers, considering factors such as demographics, needs, and purchasing behavior. Understanding your audience will help tailor your marketing efforts.

Set Marketing Goals

- **Define Objectives:** Establish clear marketing objectives, such as the desired sale price, timeline for selling, and the number of inquiries or leads you aim to generate.
- **Measure Success:** Determine how you will measure the success of your marketing efforts. This could include metrics such as the number of inquiries, viewings, offers, and the final sale price.

Develop a Marketing Budget

- **Allocate Funds:** Determine how much you are willing to spend on marketing. Consider costs for online listings, advertising, professional photography, and any other marketing activities.
- **Prioritize Expenses:** Allocate your budget based on the most effective channels for reaching your target market. Focus on high-impact, cost-effective strategies first.

Example:
Alice used social media and online listings to sell her land quickly, making a substantial profit.
Tip:
Use high-quality photos and detailed descriptions to attract buyers.

Online Listings

Utilize Real Estate Websites

- **Popular Platforms:** List your property on popular real estate websites such as Zillow, Realtor.com, and LandWatch. These platforms have a broad audience and can generate significant exposure for your listing.
- **Specialized Sites:** Consider using specialized land listing websites like LandFlip, Land And Farm, and LotNetwork, which cater specifically to land buyers and investors.

Optimize Your Listings

- **High-Quality Photos:** Use high-resolution, professional photos that showcase the property's best features. Include aerial shots if possible to give buyers a better perspective of the land.
- **Detailed Descriptions:** Write compelling descriptions that highlight the property's key features, benefits, and potential uses. Include information on zoning, utilities, access, and any unique selling points.
- **Keywords:** Use relevant keywords in your listing to improve its visibility in search results. Think about what terms potential buyers might use to find properties like yours.

Update and Monitor Listings

- **Regular Updates:** Keep your listings up to date with any changes or new information about the property. Regular updates can also improve the listing's ranking on search results.
- **Monitor Performance:** Track the performance of your listings, including the number of views, inquiries, and leads generated. Use this data to adjust your marketing strategy as needed.

Social Media Marketing

Leverage Social Media Platforms

- **Facebook:** Create a dedicated Facebook page for your real estate investments and use it to share listings, property updates, and market insights. Join local real estate and investment groups to share your listings with a targeted audience.
- **Instagram:** Use Instagram to share high-quality images and short videos of your property. Use relevant hashtags to increase visibility and reach a broader audience.
- **LinkedIn:** Utilize LinkedIn to connect with real estate professionals, investors, and potential buyers. Share your listings and engage with industry-related content to build your network.

Create Engaging Content

- **Property Tours:** Create virtual tours or walkthrough videos of your property. This can give potential buyers a better sense of the land and its features.
- **Testimonials:** Share testimonials from satisfied buyers or partners to build credibility and trust with your audience.
- **Market Insights:** Provide valuable insights and updates on the real estate market, including trends, investment tips, and local developments. This can position you as an expert in the field and attract more followers.

Run Targeted Ads

- **Facebook Ads:** Use Facebook's advertising platform to create targeted ads that reach specific demographics, locations, and interests. This can help you reach potential buyers who are most likely to be interested in your property.
- **Instagram Ads:** Run Instagram ads that showcase your property through visually appealing images and videos. Use Instagram's targeting options to reach the right audience.
- **Google Ads:** Consider running Google Ads to increase your property's visibility in search results. Target keywords related to land buying and selling to attract potential buyers actively searching for properties.

Working with Real Estate Agents

Choose the Right Agent

- **Experience and Expertise:** Look for agents who specialize in land sales and have experience in your local market. They will have a better understanding of the nuances of selling land compared to residential properties.
- **Reputation:** Check the agent's reputation by reading reviews, asking for references, and reviewing their track record of successful sales.

Collaborate on Marketing Efforts

- **Leverage Agent Networks:** Real estate agents have extensive networks of buyers, investors, and other agents. Collaborate with your agent to leverage these connections

and expand your reach.
- **Joint Marketing Plans:** Work with your agent to develop a joint marketing plan that includes both online and offline strategies. Ensure the plan aligns with your goals and target market.

Utilize Multiple Listing Service (MLS)

- **Listing Exposure:** Ensure your property is listed on the Multiple Listing Service (MLS). This platform is widely used by real estate professionals and can significantly increase your property's exposure.
- **Professional Guidance:** Your agent can provide guidance on pricing, staging, and presenting your property to attract the right buyers.

Example:

Sarah worked with a local real estate agent to market her property, leveraging the agent's network and expertise to find a buyer quickly.

Tip:

Choose an agent with experience in land sales and a strong local network.

Local Networking and Community Involvement

Attend Local Events

- **Real Estate Meetups:** Attend local real estate meetups, investment clubs, and networking events to connect with potential buyers and other investors.

- **Community Events:** Participate in community events and local business gatherings. Building relationships within the community can lead to referrals and word-of-mouth marketing.

Partner with Local Businesses

- **Contractors and Developers:** Build relationships with local contractors, builders, and developers who may be interested in purchasing land for new projects.
- **Local Businesses:** Collaborate with local businesses, such as landscaping companies, surveyors, and real estate attorneys, who can refer potential buyers to you.

Engage with the Community

- **Online Forums and Groups:** Join local online forums and social media groups related to real estate and community development. Share your listings and engage with members to build your presence.
- **Volunteer and Sponsor:** Volunteer for community projects or sponsor local events to increase your visibility and demonstrate your commitment to the community.

Example:

Tom attended local real estate meetups and built relationships with developers, leading to multiple referrals and successful sales.

Tip:

Actively engage with your local community to build relationships and generate leads.

Print and Offline Marketing

Flyers and Brochures

- **Design Quality:** Create high-quality flyers and brochures that highlight your property's features and benefits. Include professional photos, detailed descriptions, and contact information.
- **Distribution:** Distribute flyers and brochures at local real estate offices, community centers, coffee shops, and other high-traffic areas.

Yard Signs

- **Visibility:** Place clear, professional signs on the property with your contact information. Ensure the signs are visible from the road and in good condition.
- **Directional Signs:** Use directional signs to guide potential buyers to the property, especially if it is in a less visible location.

Newspaper and Magazine Ads

- **Local Publications:** Advertise in local newspapers and real estate magazines to reach a targeted audience. Highlight unique selling points and include high-quality images.
- **Niche Publications:** Consider advertising in niche publications that cater to specific buyer demographics, such as agricultural or outdoor lifestyle magazines.

Example:

David used a combination of flyers, yard signs, and newspaper ads to market his property, reaching a diverse audience and attracting multiple offers.

Tip:

Combine online and offline marketing strategies to maximize your property's exposure.

Leveraging Technology

Virtual Tours and Drone Photography

- **Virtual Tours:** Create virtual tours using 360-degree photography or video walkthroughs. This allows potential buyers to explore the property remotely.
- **Drone Photography:** Use drone photography to capture aerial views of the property. This provides a unique perspective and can highlight features like land layout and surrounding areas.

Geographic Information Systems (GIS)

- **Property Data:** Utilize GIS tools to provide detailed information about the property's location, topography, zoning, and surrounding infrastructure.
- **Interactive Maps:** Create interactive maps that potential buyers can explore online, giving them a comprehensive understanding of the property.

Real Estate Software

- **Customer Relationship Management (CRM):** Use CRM software to manage leads, track inquiries, and follow up with potential buyers. This helps streamline your marketing efforts and improve communication.
- **Marketing Automation:** Implement marketing automation tools to schedule and manage your marketing campaigns, ensuring consistent and timely communication with your audience.

Example:

Emily used drone photography and virtual tours to market her property, attracting buyers from outside the local area and increasing interest.

Tip:

Leverage technology to enhance your marketing efforts and provide potential buyers with comprehensive property information.

Case Study: Successful Marketing Campaign

Scenario:

John, a new investor, wanted to sell a piece of rural land quickly. He developed a comprehensive marketing plan to reach a broad audience.

Steps Taken:

1. **Online Listings:** John listed the property on multiple real estate websites, including Zillow, LandWatch, and Realtor.com. He used high-quality photos and a detailed

description to attract buyers.
2. **Social Media:** He created a dedicated Facebook page and Instagram profile for his real estate investments. John shared posts about the property, including virtual tours and drone footage.
3. **Local Networking:** John attended local real estate meetups and built relationships with developers and investors. He also distributed flyers and brochures at community centers and real estate offices.
4. **Professional Signage:** He placed professional yard signs on the property and used directional signs to guide potential buyers to the location.
5. **Technology:** John used CRM software to manage leads and follow up with inquiries promptly. He also created an interactive map of the property using GIS tools.

Outcome:

Within three months, John received multiple offers and sold the property for 20% above his initial asking price. His comprehensive marketing strategy ensured maximum exposure and attracted the right buyers.

Lesson Learned:

Combining online and offline marketing strategies, leveraging technology, and actively engaging with the local community can significantly increase your property's visibility and attract qualified buyers.

Conclusion

In "Use What You Don't Got to Get What You Want," we have explored various strategies and techniques to help you successfully flip land, even with limited capital. From understanding the basics of land flipping to leveraging creative financing methods and navigating legal considerations, this guide provides a comprehensive overview of the land flipping process. By learning from case studies and avoiding common pitfalls, you can maximize your profits and build a successful real estate investment portfolio.

Remember, success in land flipping requires thorough research, strategic planning, and continuous learning. Utilize the resources, tips, and examples provided in this book to enhance your knowledge and confidence in the land flipping market. With dedication and perseverance, you can achieve your financial goals and turn vacant land into profitable investments.

Thank you for reading, and best of luck in your land flipping endeavors!

Helpful Websites

Real Estate Listings and Auctions

1. **Zillow** - www.zillow.com
2. **Realtor.com** - www.realtor.com
3. **LandWatch** - www.landwatch.com
4. **Craigslist** - www.craigslist.org
5. **LoopNet** - www.loopnet.com
6. **Auction.com** - www.auction.com
7. **Bid4Assets** - www.bid4assets.com

Tax Lien and Deed Information

1. **Bid4Assets** - www.bid4assets.com (also listed under auctions)
2. **RealAuction** - www.realauction.com
3. **National Tax Lien Association** - www.ntlainfo.org

Government and Legal Resources

1. **U.S. Department of Agriculture (USDA)** - www.usda.gov
2. **Small Business Administration (SBA)** - www.sba.gov
3. **Environmental Protection Agency (EPA)** - www.epa.gov

Market Research and Data Analysis

1. **Redfin** - www.redfin.com
2. **Trulia** - www.trulia.com
3. **Reonomy** - www.reonomy.com
4. **CoreLogic** - www.corelogic.com

Financing and Crowdfunding

1. **Fundrise** - www.fundrise.com
2. **RealtyMogul** - www.realtymogul.com
3. **Patch of Land** - www.patchofland.com
4. **LendingHome** - www.lendinghome.com

Networking and Education

1. **BiggerPockets** - www.biggerpockets.com
2. **National Real Estate Investors Association (REIA)** - www.nationalreia.org
3. **Real Estate Investment Associations (REIAs)** - www.reia.org
4. **Meetup** - www.meetup.com (search for local real estate investment groups)

Tools and Services

1. **PropStream** - www.propstream.com
2. **DealMachine** - www.dealmachine.com
3. **RPR (Realtors Property Resource)** - www.narrpr.com
4. **GIS Websites** - Local county GIS websites for property data and mapping (search "[County Name] GIS")

Title and Legal Services

1. **First American Title** - www.firstam.com
2. **Fidelity National Title** - www.fntic.com
3. **Old Republic Title** - www.oldrepublictitle.com

Educational Resources and Blogs

1. **Investopedia** - www.investopedia.com
2. **The Balance** - www.thebalance.com
3. **Mashvisor Blog** - www.mashvisor.com/blog

These websites provide a variety of resources including property listings, auction details, tax lien information, market research tools, financing options, networking opportunities, and educational content. Utilizing these resources can help readers navigate the land flipping process more effectively.

www.ingramcontent.com/pod-product-compliance
Lightning Source LLC
Chambersburg PA
CBHW071838210526
45479CB00001B/198